FRAME STRUCTURES

EARLY POEMS
1974-1979

BOOKS BY SUSAN HOWE

POETRY

Hinge Picture, Telephone Books, 1974

Chanting at the Crystal Sea, Fire Exit, 1975

The Western Borders, Tuumba Press, 1976

Secret History of the Dividing Line, Telephone Books, 1978

Cabbage Gardens, Fathom Press, 1979

Pythagorean Silence, The Montemora Foundation, 1982

Defenestration of Prague, The Kulchur Foundation, 1983

Articulation of Sound Forms in Time, Awede Press, 1989

A Bibliography of the King's Book or, Eikon Basilike, Paradigm Press, 1989

The Europe of Trusts: Selected Poems, Sun & Moon Press, 1990

Singularities, Wesleyan University Press, 1990

The Nonconformist's Memorial, New Directions, 1993

CRITICISM

My Emily Dickinson, North Atlantic Books, 1985

The Birth-Mark: unsettling the wilderness in American literary history,

Wesleyan University Press, 1993

SUSAN HOWE

FRAME STRUCTURES

EARLY POEMS
1974 -1979

A NEW DIRECTIONS BOOK

ACKNOWLEDGMENTS

Some of the poems in this collection first appeared in *A Hundred Posters*, Tuumba Postcards, *Canaan*, *Personal Injury*, and *Exact Change Yearbook No. 1*. *Hinge Picture* was first published in 1974 by Telephone Books; *Chanting at the Crystal Sea* as an octavo in 1975 by Fire Exit; *Cabbage Gardens* as a pamphlet in 1979 by Fathom Press; and *Secret History of the Dividing Line* in 1978 by Telephone Books.

The engraving on page 1 of *Frame Structures* is from *Picture Book of Earlier Buffalo*, by Frank Severance (Buffalo, NY: Buffalo Historical Society Publications, Vol. 16, 1912). The principal source for *Hinge Picture* is *The Decline and Fall of the Roman Empire*, by Edward Gibbon. The photograph on page 31 of this section is from *An Introduction to Yachting*, by Frances Herreshoff (New York: Sheridan House, 1963). The photograph on page 57 of *Chanting at the Crystal Sea* and the list of names under it are from *The Gentle Americans 1864-1960: Biography of a Breed*, by Helen Howe (New York: Harper & Row, 1965). The drawing on page 73 of *Cabbage Gardens* is by Rita Lannon. The title for *Secret History of the Dividing Line* is taken from a passage heading in *History of the dividing line and other tracts. From the papers of William Byrd of Westover, in Virginia* (Richmond, 1866). A source for *Secret History of the Dividing Line* is *Touched With Fire: Civil War Letters and Diary of Oliver Wendell Holmes, Jr.*, edited by Mark DeWolfe Howe (Cambridge: Harvard University Press, 1947), and Holmes' "Memorial Day Address." The picture on page 87 of this section is from *The Practice of Perspective*, by Jean Dean Dubreuil (London: Thomas Bowles and John Bowles, 1765).

AUTHOR'S NOTE. I wrote the poems in *Cabbage Gardens* before writing most of *Secret History of the Dividing Line*. The dates on the contents page of this collection are dates of publication. —S.H.

Book design by Sylvia Frezzolini Severance
Manufactured in the United States of America
New Directions Books are printed on acid-free paper.
First published as New Directions Paperbook 822 in 1996
Published simultaneously in Canada by Penguin Books Canada Limited

Library of Congress Cataloging in Publication

Howe, Susan.
    Frame structures: early poems, 1974-1979 / Susan Howe.
        p.   cm.
    ISBN 0-8112-1322-6 (pbk.)
    I. Title.
PS3558.0893A6   1996
811' .54—dc20   95-46418
                                                                      CIP

New Directions Books are published for James Laughlin
by New Directions Publishing Corporation,
80 Eighth Avenue, New York 10011

CONTENTS

FRAME STRUCTURES

THE SECOND OLDEST VIEW OF BUFFALO

PUBLISHED IN PHILADELPHIA, 1845, FROM AN ORIGINAL SKETCH BY LT. JESSE D. ELLIOTT, ACCOMPANYING HIS REPORT TO THE
SECRETARY OF THE NAVY ON THE CAPTURE OF THE DETROIT AND CALEDONIA, DATED BLACK ROCK, OCT. 9, 1812.

Flanders

On Sunday, December 7, 1941, I went with my father to the zoo in Delaware Park even now so many years after there is always for me the fact of this treasured memory of togetherness before he enlisted in the army and went away to Europe. On that Sunday in Buffalo the usually docile polar bears roved restlessly back and forth around the simulated rocks caves and waterfall designed to keep brute force fenced off even by menace of embrace so many zoo animals are accounted fierce. I recall there were three though I could be wrong because I was a deep and nervous child with the north wind of the fairy story ringing in my ears as well as direct perception. Three bears running around rocks as if to show how modern rationalism springs from barbarism and with such noise to call out boldly boldly ventured is half won. Three bears splashing each other and others gathered at the iron railing as though we hadn't been enjoying liberty its checks and balances. Daddy held on tightly to my hand because animals do communicate in a state resembling dissociation so a prepared people will rid the settlement of ice deities identified with rivers they cause animism. Everyone talking of war in those days. Enough to weigh against love. Animals sense something about ruin I think he said our human spirits being partly immaterial at that prefigured time though we didn't know then how free will carries us past to be distance waiting for another meeting a true relation.

Historical imagination gathers in the missing

Primitive Notions I

John Adams comes in second.

After his appointment as President of the Continental Board of War and Ordance, the constitutional lawyer helped Thomas Jefferson and Benjamin Franklin to draft a Declaration of Independence in the service of liberty and equality. His not being able to see why no one who is not an owner can be recognized by law to be a possessor

a parent figure scattered among others in favor of disobedience. "Well goodbye and don't forget me."

In 1779 Adams was chosen as minister plenipotentiary for negotiating a treaty of peace and another treaty of commerce with Great Britain. He remained in Europe for several years with his two sons, John Quincy and Charles, for company. Abigail Adams was left behind in Braintree, Massachusetts, with their daughter Nabby, and youngest son Thomas. Most of the absent statesman's business abroad was divided between London and Paris though Adams also spent some months in the Netherlands where he had been authorized to conduct similar diplomatic arrangements. After months of negotiations, memorials, categorical answers, ceremonial visits, "innumerable vexations," travels between cities and provinces, even an illness so severe he lay in a coma for five days, his Dutch mission succeeded remarkably well. On February 26, 1782, the Provincial states of Friesland voted to instruct their deputies in the States General to recognize the United States as an independent government. On March 28, the other states of Holland followed suit. On April 19, the States General of the United Netherlands resolved "that Mr. Adams shall be admitted and acknowledged in Quality of Envoy of the United States of North America to their High Mightinesses, as he is admitted and acknowledged by the present." In September 1782, the Dutch treaty was formally approved, signed, and sealed, along with a treaty of amity and commerce. "My loan," Adams wrote in relation to the commerce part, "is considered not only as a new one but as entering deep into the essence of all the present political systems of the world and no man dares engage in it until it is clearly determined what characters will bear rule and what system is to prevail in this country."

A flow of capital from the Netherlands across the Atlantic Ocean follows.

Bailment

In 1792 a group of wealthy gentlemen, members of six Dutch banking houses based in Amsterdam, pooled their money to found a real estate consortium known as the Holland Land Company. Five commissioners, Wilhelm Willink, Nicolaas Van Staphorst, Christiaan Van Eeghen, Hendrick Vollenhoven, and R. J. Schimmelpennick, under the directorship of Stadnitski and Son, represented the six houses. Together they agreed to purchase huge undeveloped tracts, then referred to as "wild lands," in the central and western parts of New York and Pennsylvania as a business speculation. While the consortium pledged their reputation, through sales of stock in American securities, to Dutch citizens at home for the recovery of capital with the largest attainable profit possible, a smaller Club of Three (Van Eeghen, Ten Cate, and Vollenhoven) managed land ventures abroad. Their plan was to sell the wild lands to multitudes of German, Scottish, and Irish settlers, many of them poor and desperate, who were also rushing, under nobody's auspices, crossing from one field of force to another field of force.

In relation to relief not to be treated as hollow and a negative.

How many Netherlanders actually bought these shares? The records are scant. Most remained bracketed with the original purchasers, or their heirs. Other more general Holland Land Company manuscripts have been carefully preserved here and in Amsterdam. Eventually the Company acquired and surveyed five and a half million acres in central and western New York and Pennsylvania. The Dutch gentlemen bankers, now absentee landlords, left the management of these vast back country tracts in the hands of a few carefully selected agents responsible for surveying the holdings, then selling them at retail, often on credit, to settlers. Theophile Cazenove, a Dutch entrepreneurial protégé of Sadnitski, was sent across the ocean bearing letters of introduction to various well-heeled American gentlemen bankers, among them Andrew Craigie in New York. Other special agents followed, including Paul Busti, an Italian resident of Holland and brother-in-law of Vollenhoven's banking partner. Even before the American Revolution proprietors of early settlement were buying backlands to hold for a rise in value.

Federalism: its breadth and all-embracing perspective. Lines represent the limits of bodies encompassed by the eye.

Floating loans
Joseph Ellicott, sometimes called "the father of Buffalo," was born in Bucks County, Pennsylvania, in 1760 to Quaker parents from England. The Holland Land Company tested him first as an explorer in the East Allegheny region. Next they had him surveying lands around the Genesee River until in 1800 he was appointed by Paul Busti to serve as agent for the Dutch in the Genesee for six years. Two years later Ellicott's agency was increased to include all Dutch holdings in western New York. By the summer of 1802, largely due to this surveyor's aggressively acquisitive talents, the western portion of New York State was set off as an independent county. Between civil and criminal dollar windfalls the life of common law is experience. For the next twenty-one years, often heroically improvising, Ellicott as company surveyor and resident subagent, controlled land sales, tenant relations, the location of counties, towns, villages, and political negotiations with the state legislature. Until his forced retirement in 1821 he wielded immense political influence over thousands of settlers many of them debtors. I learned about him from out-of-print records and journals published by local antiquarian societies.

Land speculators, surveyors, promoters, publicists, and primitive judges were extraordinarily free in terms of strategic flight into the wilderness. If one sticks to the letter, now where are their names indexed? The only detailed study focused on the ground, the base, the frame, of prevailing social and economic systems in the backlands of western Pennsylvania and upper western New York State during the heady days of the early Republic, I have been able to find this summer, is *The Holland Land Company,* by Paul Demund Evans, published by the Buffalo Historical Society in 1924. Evans' book went out of print long ago but it's still in the stacks of the Sterling Memorial Library. According to the recall card on the back jacket *The Holland Land Company* has been taken out four times since 1977 in spite of the flowering of New Historicism.

In most towns in New York State there were no hearses until around 1830. The dead were borne on a shoulder bier sometimes for many miles. Members of the funeral procession carried staffs, halberts, badges of authority while they walked to the accompaniment of a tolling bell to the grave. Theophile Cazenove, Paul Busti, Robert Morris, Jan Linklaen, Gerrit Boon, David A. Ogden, Judge Wilson, Joseph Ellicott, and the problem of distance.

I was never sure what my father was doing in the army. Then I was never sure of anything what with his rushing away our changing cities and World War banging at windows the boundless phenomena of madness. I remember him coming back to Buffalo from basic training by snapshot once or twice in a uniform. Absence is always present in a picture in its right relation. There is a split then how to act. Laws are relations among individuals.

When Theophile Cazenove reached America in 1789, he realized that Philadelphia was the best scene for his operations because the future of American funds, federal and state, depended on the actions of the federal government. Pavements were in wider space and getting social satisfaction he carried along a letter of introduction from his backers in Amsterdam to Andrew Craigie in New York. The Van Staphorts told Craigie their envoy came to America "to gratify his thirst after knowledge in order to become better acquainted with the Genius of their Government and the objects of their growing commerce."

In the cold drama of moral lucidity there is primitive reason just as in the calm dicta of moral lucidity there is personal reason.

Women and children experience war and its nightmare. Their war-dreams share with dreams of other kinds that they are occurrences full of blown sand seaward foam in which disappearance fields expression. If fire drives out fire so does pity pity beside

variant unabridged bits, mortal and menacing, anything but pliable and apart.

Clouds must have come under the western edge of the old suspension bridge. Debris thrown down during construction has nearly filled the intervening ever-flowing current

architecture of paved distances prolonged into the sealed cars speeding along Scajaquada Creek Expressway to the suburbs.

Craigie Circle

In 1942 my mother, younger sister Fanny, and I left Buffalo to live in Cambridge, Massachusetts, so we would be close to her aunt and uncle who lived near Harvard Square, and to my father's sister and father in Boston. We moved into a ground floor apartment at 6 Craigie Circle. Craigie Circle is a small deadend road where Craigie and Berkeley streets intersect near Huron Avenue. Huron refers either to an Indian tribe or to the second largest of the Great Lakes the one just north of Lake Erie or to both at once. Berkeley is named for the Anglo-Irish bishop and philosopher author of *Principles of Human Knowledge* among many other works and Craigie for Andrew Craigie whose activities as Apothecary-General of the Revolutionary Army and other speculations made him rich for a time. Probably Andrew was Cazenove's New York contact and even if Craigie was another Andrew coincidence produces an optical ghost or guess so here he is now. After the revolution, Vassall House (the largest mansion on Tory Row) built in 1759 by John Vassall, a Loyalist who returned to England during the Revolution, was renamed Craigie when Mr. and Mrs. Craigie acquired it. Tory Row (previously the King's Highway) became Brattle Street. The banker died bankrupt but his widow, Elizabeth Nancy Shaw Craigie from Nantucket (now bald but wearing a turban and perpetually studying Spinoza), managed to hang on to her home. Some Vassalls are buried in Cambridge churchyard under a stone inscribed with only picture-writing ((a goblet and a sun)) (((Vas-sol)))). Mrs. Craigie supported herself by letting rooms. In 1837 when William Wadsworth Longfellow, the newly appointed Smith Professor of French and Spanish at Harvard

College, became one of her lodgers, he rented the room once occupied by George Washington (another parent figure) at the beginning of the Revolution when he planned and commanded the siege of Boston. Longfellow was an early pioneer in establishing modern languages as a discipline in American education but whatever contribution the poet-professor made to anything had been relegated to minor (even laughingstock) status by contemporary critical theorists of both Cambridges during the 1930s and 1940s. When I.A. Richards (affectionately called I.A.R. by initiates in reference to *Coleridge* ((S.T.C.)) *on Imagination*) whose early managerial replotting of the literary ground plan in *Principles of Literary Criticism* (1924), *Practical Criticism: A Study of Literary Judgment* (1929), and currently *Basic English and its Use* (1943), sagely observed, "few things are worse than *Hiawatha* or *The Black Cat, Lorna Doone,* or *Le Crime de Sylvestre Bonnard,*" and used "In the Churchyard at Cambridge" ("a stock exercise in provincial sanctimony") as graphic illustration of an extremely bad poem in the pages of *Practical Criticism;* it was all over for the first author on I.A.R.'s proscribed list for the time being. The waters of the Atlantic closed over the Wreck of the Hesperus. Once, after quoting the French proverb, "it is not enough to be a great man—you must also come at the right time," Longfellow is said to have paused before adding, "this is particularly true of authors."

"Between the dark and the daylight/When the night is beginning to lower,/Comes a pause in the day's occupations/That is known as the Children's Hour." During the 1940s in what seemed to be a running gag at faculty gatherings "children's" became "cocktail" as if the mere word-change brought all adults involved in the machinery of aesthetic distinctions happily together in order to exchange signals somehow beyond our apprehension the implication being children of modernists were perfectly free to get lost at six.

"Daddy loved animals more than people," is still a family saying. In 1945, after he came back from the war, we had two dachshunds because he couldn't bear to be without a dog. The first one Waddy, short for Wadsworth Longfellow, marked the correspondence between waddling and poetry. Waddy was followed by Minny, short for Minnehaha Laughing Water, because she peed everywhere and we couldn't train her; uncontrollable literary production encompassed unsuccessful bowel training. Even if the real Minnehaha does almost nothing in *The Song of Hiawatha* the poem itself has inspired more parodies than any other in the English language.

In 1843, when Longfellow married Frances Elizabeth Appleton, her father, a wealthy Boston industrialist, bought Craigie House and eight acres of meadow adjoining it for the couple. In 1943 the meadows were almost all houses or paved over because privacy depends on a one-sided way. Craigie House renamed Longfellow hadn't been ideally rearranged as a museum it was only half over. Henry Longfellow Dana was living in one part of the house, with a lover, while Charles and Helen Hopkinson (also Longfellow descendants) often occupied the other. A caretaker (the position traditionally went to a poet or a Divinity School student) lived in the attic. Sometimes the three of us had Sunday dinner with the Hopkinsons usually after accompanying Aunt Muriel (then referred to by children on her block as "the witch," she was one of the first women to earn a degree from Trinity College, Dublin) and vague Arthur Darby Nock (bachelor scholar of ancient history known for standing on his head naked in his rooms at Eliot House; when he died he requested that he be buried at Aunt Muriel's feet so they remain close in Mount Auburn Cemetery) to hear Uncle Willy deliver his weekly sermon at Harvard's Memorial Chapel. (Her name was Muriel Bennett when she met Willard Sperry at Oxford where he was a Rhodes scholar. They married and moved to Fall River, Massachusetts, where he became a Congregational minister. Fall River was horribly dull except for Lizzie Borden a neighbor they remembered peering into their daughter Henrietta's pram. Thankfully they left Fall River quickly because he became Dean of the Harvard Theological School and moved to Cambridge where my mother came to visit them and met my father before the war.) When such Sundays loomed into view Fanny and I sat at the front of Memorial Chapel beside the great person of great-aunt Muriel. She tried every covert trick in her book to make us laugh out loud while great-uncle Willy wrapped in his great black robe was going on about something holy oh she was serious in regard to us and all the people listening. Later we might sit in the dining room of Longfellow House eating lunch on one side of a roped-off area while the resident poet-caretaker guided sightseers single-file along the other side of the barrier pointing out ornaments, furnishings, portraits, structural details; as if we were ghosts. If private space is the space of private writing, objects must be arranged in position (witnesses and vanishing points) not looking both ways at once. Something about nature "nice" children good manners in architecture. Space is a frame we map ourselves in.

When B.F. Skinner asks, "Why write sonnets rather than maxims, aphorisms, letters, or short essays? What is to be gained from dancing in chains?" the father of American Behaviorism is referring to Shakespeare's sonnet 129 and I.A. Richards' "Jakobson's Shakespeare: the Subliminal Structures of a Sonnet," at once. I found Skinner's essay published in *I.A.*

Richards: Essays in his Honor. "The linguist's 'deep structure,' like Freud's 'depth psychology,' is a spatial metaphor which serves several functions. It is useful in referring to the visibility of behavioral processes and their effects and the role played by visibility in the determination of behavior; it should not, of course, be used to suggest that an analysis is profound rather than superficial." This section of the behaviorial psychologist's conclusion is enclosed in parentheses. A footnote says the paper's preparation was funded by a Career Award from the National Institutes of Mental Health. My sister Fanny remembers her fear of open spaces between Berkeley and Huron because somewhere close to us the Skinners' daughters were being brought up in boxes. When the boxes called air-cribs were put outside for air she thought she saw internal objects. I must have blocked them out.

Between Berkeley Street and Brattle some meticulous gardens still remained among lawns abandoned to children some even wilder patches of weed and brush. In those early days language was always changing. Faded words fell like dead leaves in a closed circle moving toward the mind but we didn't know we were born because deep down there is no history. Boundaries interlinking public and private are very well, precaution and policy, thought is arranged over this, the property of *h* (breath without sound) comes between *g* and *t* (sound without breath) in daughter slaughter laughter. Letters launched into space rush one child to the next, more or less at large, acting wolves and tigers, colliding with landowners (by subterfuge). By controlled experiment B(urrhus), F(rederic) Skinner proved pigeons could play Ping-Pong. Not behaving. Not earning a living. Not to be afraid of everything passing those buildings; the obstinate repetition of doors and windows. No, there were footpaths we used as shortcuts going from home to school and home again. "This is the forest primeval. The murmuring pines and the hemlocks,/Bearded with moss, and in garments green, indistinct in the twilight," half-forgotten neighboring backlands recover breaks and zigzags, ranges of feeling, little maneuvers in distance perception. "Where is the thatch-roofed village, the home of Acadian farmers,—"

Berkeley, Brattle, Craigie, Buckingham, Huron; it was Nathaniel Hawthorne who passed on the Acadian story of feminine faithfulness and wandering that became *Evangeline,* he heard it from a friend who heard it from Mrs. George Haliburton, a French Canadian deported from Nova Scotia, along with three thousand fellow Acadians, in 1755. Mrs. Haliburton was living in exile in Boston when she told the story. *Evangeline* is the first long poem in North American literature inspired by New World themes, stories, and history to live beyond the time frame of its composition. Who except wretched schoolchildren now reads Longfellow?" asks Ludwig Lewisohn in *Expression in America*, as if rapid reading is really divination. Evangeline, daughter of Acadie, a kindred spirit of Saint Eulalie patroness of landless sailors, loses her lover Gabriel during the prevailing disorder the tumult and stir of embarking.

"Eveline! Evvy!"

"I am writing a series of epiclets—ten—for a paper. . . . I call the series *Dubliners* to betray the soul of that hemiplegia or paralysis which many consider a city." "Eveline" is the fourth story in *Dubliners* though James Joyce wrote it second after he finished writing "The Sisters" and met Nora Barnacle in 1904. Eveline's lover Frank is a sailor, he will rescue her from home; they will be exiles together and live in Argentina. "Come!—" he calls to her. All the seas of the world tumble about Eveline's heart she cannot or will not leave home because of a promise to her dead mother. He rushes beyond the barrier and calls her to follow. Systems preserve and nurse their traditions. "So unto separate ships were Basil and Gabriel carried./While in despair on the shore Evangeline stood with her father." My mother, Mary Manning, was born in Dublin, in 1905. When she was a child her father was almost always living in another country and his father before him.

"—Derevaun Seraun! Derevaun Seraun!"

Nigeria was named for the Royal Niger Company, a private organization established to meet the requirements of British trade along Africa's third largest river during the European "scramble for Africa" of the 1880s. In 1900 French, German, and English possessions in that part of West Africa were demarcated after much quarreling. Ensuing complications (wars with various Muslim rulers in the interior, disputes on the western frontier with France) were finally too much for the resources of a private company to handle. The word "royal" was dropped and the company surrendered its charter, transferring all political rights to the crown. Irony is saying one thing while meaning another. Nigeria became another British "protectorate."

John Fitzmaurice Manning (1871–1920) was Anglo-Irish and a younger son. In the schema of colonialism he didn't have many career options neither did his father a colonel in the British army who first served at Halifax in Nova Scotia and later at the British army camp in the Curragh, County Kildare. That John Manning also died young also leaving a shabby genteel widow with several shabby genteel children. In 1885 the

European powers partioned what land was still theoretically unclaimed in the African continent. The British occupation of Nigeria began in earnest in 1897. Trained as a doctor my grandfather was one of those members of the Colonial Service assigned "to open the country for civilized occupation." I still have his copy of Swinburne's poems. He has signed his name on the flyleaf inside; "J. Manning, Lagos. 1897." In 1903 the capital city of Kano, a walled fortified town then under the control of a Muslim sultan, was defeated by a British assault. I think that's where he worked most of the time. My grandmother went several times to visit him there though she never took the children; sickness mortality and the heat. In a sepia photograph the couple are standing in a field in front of the hospital at Kano. It's a long building like ones in *The African Queen* and various other fiction films. Seen at a distance their expressions are hard to determine. Both wear wide-brimmed sunhats. He is tall, very thin, and somewhat stooped. But he has a way of standing with one knee bent and his right foot turned in just the way my mother and I stand sometimes. Once every two years he came home to Dublin on leave for six months. My mother says her mother loved another man anyway but he was a Catholic so Susan Bennett married Protestant John Fitzmaurice Manning on the rebound. When she died in her eighties the other man's picture was beside her bed. If this is true I wonder if anyone has paid attention to the many marginal markings in *Swinburne,* the only book of his I have seen over here. "Yea, hope at highest and all her fruit,/And time at fullest and all his dower,/I had given you surely, and life to boot,/Were we once made one for a single hour./ But now, you are twain, you are cloven apart,/Flesh of his flesh, but heart of my heart; /And deep in one is the bitter root,/And sweet for one is the lifelong flower." He has underlined "flesh" "flesh" and "heart of my heart" and drawn a pencil slash down the right hand margin of this stanza from "The Triumph of Time." Their marriage produced two daughters and a son. Irrelevant, eccentric, cross; when he did come home he drank and was bad tempered so they didn't miss him when he left again. Leaving leaving arriving arriving. Even a civilized person will kick a door whatever the policy if modernity surrounds every threshold point of contact. She remembers one summer he was home and they were all together visiting Fitzmaurice relations in Kerry. Three telegrams were delivered by donkey cart. Her father and his two brothers packed and left immediately. It was August, 1914.

"NIGERIA. A British protectorate in West Africa occupying the lower basin of the Niger and the country between that river and Lake Chad, including the Fula empire (*i.e.* the Hausa States) and the greater part of Bornu. It embraces most of the territory in the square formed by the meridians of 3° and 14° E., and the parallels of 4° and 14° N., and has an area of about 338,000 sq.m. The Protectorate is bounded W., N. and N.E. by French possessions (Dahomey, Upper Senegal and Niger Colony, and Chad territory), S.E. by the German colony of Cameroon and S. by the Atlantic. This is how volume XIX MUN to ODDFELLOWS of the eleventh edition of the *Encyclopaedia Britannica* puts it three years before uncontrollable modernity before the whole world goes wild.

"NIGER, a great river of West Africa, inferior only to the Congo and Nile among the rivers of the continent, and the only river in Africa which, by means of its tributary the Benue, affords a waterway uninterrupted by rapids, and available for shallow-draught steamers to the far interior. NIAGARA, a river of North America, running northward from Lake Erie to Lake Ontario, and carrying the discharge of all the Laurentian or Great Lakes excepting Lake Ontario."

Clans and individuals adopt the name of animals cities seldom do. Prefaces are usually afterimages.

Lackawanna could be be considered the offshoot of an instinct for preservation because orders from European countries for steel products during the First World War turned what had been a company steel town or labor camp consisting of Poles, Russians, Hungarians, Italians, Bulgarians, Spaniards, and Arabs into a sub-city of Buffalo named for a company. Most of the steelworkers were from Eastern Europe. They poured in hoping to go home sometime. A crowd of fifty thousand people jammed the meadow in Delaware Park, after Woodrow Wilson's declaration of war on April 2, 1917, because three thousand local conscripts were bound the other way. To say goodbye

During the 1850s when the Niagara's water power was harnessed and the city's position between action and desire guaranteed its preeminence as the major inland port in the United States, Buffalo was a rail center and highway crossroads for hauling tonnages of grain, limestone, coal, iron, ore, lumber, petroleum, and railroad cars all over the place. Many materials of everyday life were made of iron in Buffalo. In 1851 the first rail line, operated by the Delaware, Lackawanna and Western Railroad Company, linked Buffalo with the coal fields of the southern tier of the state and three years after this the Buffalo and Pittsburgh Railroad connected to the coal fields of western Pennsylvania so the iron trade really took off. Soon comes electricity and the Great National Exchange. Wars have also been good for the city. In *High Hopes: The Rise and Decline of Buffalo, New York,*

Mark Goodman shows how the Civil War strengthened commerce thus giving birth to industry while the Spanish-American War inspired patriotic fervor thus giving birth to the Pan American Exposition of 1901 where displays of electricity, particularly the Electric Tower, attracted thousands of summer visitors and President McKinley was assassinated by an anarchist. The assassin, Leon Czolgosz, told police the words of Emma Goldman set him on fire.

I knew the story of Fanny Appleton Longfellow's death by fire, on the 4th of July, 1861, because of a little blue parasol in my American grandfather's apartment. She had taken it along to shade her face from the sun when she went out to Quincy earlier the same summer to visit my great-grandparents. They kept her sunshade as a memento. Eventually it came to my grandmother Fanny Quincy, maybe because of her name. When she died young, Grandpa took it with him to Louisburg Square. Mary Elizabeth Manning Howe Adams passed along Francis Elizabeth Appleton Longfellow's faded and tattered sunshade to the National Park Service in 1995. The Park Service manages the Longfellow House now it is a museum.

Independence Day. She is sitting near an open window in the family library. There is a meadow outside where her children often play. It's midsummer they are probably around somewhere. She has cut small locks of hair from her two younger daughters is using sealing wax to close these souvenirs of love in boxes. Two doctrines materialism and spiritualism. The objects which surround my body those which are near to my body frame a simple idea of time. As shadows wait on the sun so a shot soul falling shot leaves its body fathomless to draw it out. The armies are tired of their terrible mismanagement not counting the missing. Envelopes and boxes are often metaphorically linked with motherly contrivance. Domesticity is in her hands so of course these are arranged; picked for her children's children to touch and be touched. Quickly quickly it has all been too easy. Wisdom is a defense and money is a defense. Knowledge knowledge to the last grain of economic innocence. Will you come back so far to show us the cost? You ask if the universe only exists in thought, creative and subtle? Flame is not impalpable. She is using a lighted match to melt the wax has already begun to recover the refuse. Don't you remember the essence of English idealism? The wax is here just so things *are*.

A spark from a match maybe hot wax ignites her flowing muslin summer dress. Her husband, sleeping in his study nearby, his custom always, hears short phrases not words. Compare the phenomenon of sleeping with the phenomenon of burning. I suppose him a great distance off in pastures detached from memory. Enveloped in flame she runs into vision a succession of static images a single unbroken movement under her breath "dead woman" she bats at wing strokes. Arcadia Accadia L'Acadie sea birds clang. Why can't he see that the loved object will perish? Well we don't see dark spaces between film frames, why, because of persistence of vision. God's sun-clothed bride wades backward white petticoat tabernacle body as in a dream I perceive distance a great way off. She grips him. Print your symptoms of melancholia on a sheet of paper in a singsong manner now get better. He tries. Tries to smother the flames by wrapping her in any near cloth object such as a mat or rug. Fire badly burns his face and hands but he would rather be burned than buried. Long ago open fireplaces invited guests to enjoy the warmth of huge wood fires; candles and primitive lamps provided some escape from the immediacy of lived experience. Stricken out of the cloud-folds of her garment shaken she suffers intensely for a short time then gets put to sleep with ether so she wakes up calm and free of pain. Edenic mapping of the New World Acadie. Softly softly hear the noise of distant falls of many wars and wars for national independence.

In 1920 my Irish grandfather was discharged from the British Colonial Service and came home to Ireland for good: "disabled from war wounds" is how my mother puts it but World War I was over and the few other people who know anything about him say "alcoholism." When he died in Dublin after a short illness or something else he was forty-nine. The children were sent away during this illness or whatever it was. The surface of life closed over his impecunious unutterable case; so the effect is secrecy though not in the sense of a crime. I wish I knew him as an adequate over-the-sea relation but I only imagine distancing maneuvers. In one torn photograph he is standing alone wearing a heavy overcoat in the back garden at 35 Wellington Place. It's a haggard profile shot. Sometimes my ninety-year-old mother lives over her life as if I were the other Susan Manning. Sometimes her father comes close and close. So there are two images. Two phases of thought many miles apart. She remembers a few wood carvings he brought home with him their strangeness. Fragmentary deities indwelling spirits of the dead, wraiths, a mask in one piece, soft wood black-red ocher white coating, eyelets pierced in the wood, another ancestor ritual figure, oak blackened by fire; she says when everything was still to come he wanted to be in the arts he was just miscast. She has kept a few of his early pencil sketches as if pieces of tenderness chipped off by a hair's breadth.
  I hope you cleared the threshold, lived on into it, to yourself.

When we lived on Craigie Circle, Mary Manning (Howe) was already the Irish author of three plays, *Youth's the Season?*, *Storm Over Wicklow*, and *Happy Families*. In Buffalo she wrote a novel called *Mount Venus*. She was also the drama director for both the Idler Club at Radcliffe College, then a place for the daughters of educated men, and the Harvard Dramatic Club, because their regular director, a man, was overseas in the fighting. I can't remember the first play she directed but I remember the Agassiz Theatre and how frivolous the name Idler seemed in wartime most of all the heavy curtain in itself a spectacle whose task it was to open at a certain moment in connection with distancing tactics directed by my mother. Her thought over here mapping the deep area where no stage set was ever permanent actors being one character then another according to movements she blocked out. Actors speaking correctly from memory. Trying to separate and distinguish what *is* recollection as detached from memory keeping falsity hidden. The smell of make-up the shrouded sets and props.

During the early 1930s when my father was a graduate student at Harvard Law School, he was one of a special group Professor Felix Frankfurter referred to as "my boys." Frankfurter's role as interpreter of the Court and the Constitution, and advisor to President Roosevelt, partly depended on the work of these students, disciples, and protégés, who later, through his influence, obtained crucial positions in New Deal Washington and came to be known as "Hot Dogs." Frankfurter also had academic dogs. When Buffalo University, inspired and advised by Frankfurter, was establishing a law school, Louis Jaffe, Ernest Griswold, and my father were more or less ordered there in 1937. When Justice Oliver Wendell Holmes, Jr. died in 1935 his papers had been placed in charge of his executor John Gorham Palfrey. Palfrey made them available to Felix Frankfurter because Frankfurter was Holmes' original choice to write his authorized biography. In 1939 Frankfurter was appointed to the Supreme Court of the United States and no longer had the time or inclination to undertake the monumental task of sorting through his wordy predecessor's papers so he chose my father, who had been Holmes' law clerk and secretary in 1933-34, to do the job. Most of the papers were at Harvard and after he came home from serving overseas in 1946 we never went back to Buffalo. Frankfurter must have helped to arrange his appointment to the Harvard Law School, where he joined the teaching faculty as the first Charles Warren Professor in the History of American Law. Griswold was also recalled from Buffalo. He became the Dean, and Louis Jaffe followed in their wake. As well as teaching, my father immediately began work on the biography *he* may not have had time nor inclination to write. Considerate and reasonable with a streak of radicalism, he was a man of common sense, a lover of learning, able and good. But something in him, unexorcised though caged for the short range, made him work without rest, never letting on to those close to him what the cost might be. When he died, suddenly and unexpectedly in 1967, he was only sixty. "From the first I was subject to pressures to have Mark get on with his work on Holmes," Griswold somewhat regretfully noted at the memorial service. G. Edward White, in the bibliographic essay appended to *Justice Oliver Wendell Holmes: Law and the Inner Self* (1993), refers to my father as "Felix Frankfurter's 'authorized' narrator of the legend of Holmes."

Touched With Fire: The Civil War Letters and Diary of Oliver Wendell Holmes, Jr. 1861-1864, edited by Mark DeWolfe Howe, was published by Harvard University Press in 1947. When the Second World War was over the male director of Harvard's Dramatic Club also returned to Radcliffe and my mother was out of work until the first real Brattle Theatre (not cinema) began. We left the apartment on Craigie Circle, moved to a house on Appleton Street, and my sister Helen was born.

Once every week my father visited his mother's eccentric widowed sister, Mabel Davis. By 1947 she was was more than eccentric. She lived in Boston in a suite at the rapidly decaying residential Hotel Lenox, lovingly cared for by an elderly French seamstress who had been with her for over forty years, most of them spent in Argentina, where her husband, Walter Gould Davis, was the director of the Argentine Meteorological Service. Aunt Mabel no longer remembered any of our names but she was, in her own oblique way, sharp as a tack. Each week with utmost civility she greeted the nephew whose name she had forgotten with the same salutation: "Give me your paw Attorney at Law".

The Proving Years (1963) is the second volume of my father's authorized biography of Oliver Wendell Holmes Jr. He called the first chapter "The Stars and the Plough" probably because that's the title of *The Plough and the Stars*. Sean O'Casey's play about the Easter Rising, named for the symbol on the flag of the Irish citizen army, is one of my mother's favorites. The stars are the ideal the plough reality. I guess my father meant to put reality first.

The Angel in the Library

Antiquarianism is as old as historical writing even if Francis Bacon in *The Advancement of Learning* defines antiquities as: "history defaced or some remnants of history which have casually escaped the shipwreck of time." The patriotic zeal of local antiquarian scholarship is often doctrinal it confirms a community's need to flatter current misconceptions. According to genteel tradition Buffalo could be a mispronunciation for "beau-fleuve" because French trappers traders and Jesuit missionaries were the first European settlers to stop in common identity where the present breaks in. In *Gibbon and His Roman Empire*, David P. Jordan shows the ways *The Decline and Fall of the Roman Empire* was partially built on the research of sceptics and historical Pyrrhonists outside the universities. Pyrrhonists were usually proud to be called amateurs. Often their research developed out of a need to classify their own collections of coins, statues, vases, inscriptions, emblems, etc.; and the work demanded new tactics. Gibbon calls the literary results of the labors of these dilettante researchers the "subsidiary rays" of history. The best known defender of uncertainty in history, Pierre Bayle, depended heavily on the work of antiquarians. Studies of medals and inscriptions were more reliable less subject to human corruption, he felt. Bayle's first idea wasn't to write an encyclopedia of knowledge rather he hoped to produce a record of mistakes. On May 22, 1692, he told a friend: "I formed a plan to compose a *Critical Dictionary* which would contain a collection of the mistakes which have been made by compilers of dictionaries as well as other writers, and which would summarize under each name of a man or a city the mistakes concerning that man or that city." Bayle's *Historical and Critical Dictionary* follows the spirit of coordination's lead rather than a definite plan. Trivial curiosities and nonsensical subjects are kernels to be collated like tunes for a fact while important matters are neglected. A perfect history is "unacceptable to all sects and nations; for it is a sign that the writer neither flatters nor spares any of them." This sceptical aphorism can be found under the heading "An Explanation Concerning Obscenities."

Documentary histories, registers, and catalogues, often lovingly gathered by local amateurs, tend to be filed, boxed, sheltered: shut up. What is it about *documents* that seems to require their relegation to the bedroom (a private place) as if they were bourgeois Victorian women? Honored, looked to for advice, shielded from the rabble by guardians of "tradition"/"aesthetic taste," available only to particular researchers (husbands or bachelor machines) and caretakers (librarians cataloguers secretaries) so long as they are desirable (readable not too tattered) capable of bearing children (articles chapters books) rearing them (aiding research), they remain sheltered at home (museum collections libraries). *This doesn't only apply to the papers of some cultural icons who walk abroad the windows all open as to what is being said from a great distance flesh and blood yes human from head to foot so that we cannot reinter them beyond and apart.* Recently while backtracking through the authorized edition of John Adams' *Diaries* I was struck by a reproduction of an early American painting, "Congress Voting Independence," and thought I might use it on the cover of this book. A footnote cited "Congress Voting Independence: The Trumbull and Pine-Savage Paintings," by James M. Mulcahy in the *Pennsylvania Magazine of History and Biography*, 80: 74-9 (January 1956). When I went in search of it in the stacks in Sterling I found the right shelf but all issues of the periodical had been removed to the Franklin Collection Room, a place so far unknown to me, a room on the second floor. Here Yale University's custodians of early American culture sequester whatever back-issues of periodicals, local histories, antiquarian studies, bibliographies, even obliquely concern Benjamin Franklin or Philadelphia I'm not sure which because so many people consider both man and city as ideal stand-ins for America's Age of Reason. Franklin often veiled himself under an array of allegorical aliases ("Father Abraham," "Silence Doogood," "a certain public-spirited Gentleman," "the clean plain old Man with white Locks") as if he already felt the snooping future and must artfully prepare his face in advance. The materials are arranged according to a certain scheme of order I couldn't make out. A librarian, seated near the entrance at a desk piled high with papers and catalogues, asked me to produce credentials i.e., write my university affiliation on a list along with my reason for being there. I produced the required proof of professional departmentalization so she brought me the "Congress Voting Independence" piece. Mulcahy referred to two other articles by someone called Hart. I decided to continue postponing my cover idea because it was a hot midsummer day the Benjamin Franklin Room doesn't have air conditioning and the librarian looked impatient. I knew that even if one of the Harts was in *The Pennsylvania Magazine of History and Biography*, XXIX (1905) I would still have to locate the room where bound volumes of *The Proceedings of the Massachusetts Historical Society* are currently being sheltered from the public gaze, to find the other.

Borne on the bier with white and bristly beard

My American grandfather, Mark Antony DeWolfe Howe (1864–1960), was an antiquarian. In the 1940s the term "antiquarian" already suggested faded secondhand bookshops and useless scholarship. Mark Antony was named for his father Mark Antony DeWolfe Howe (1808–1895). This primal Mark Antony, somewhat scornfully referred to as "The Bishop" by his three Bostonian grandchildren (two atheists one Jungian), was ordained into the Episcopal ministry in the early 1830s, and served as rector in various churches in Boston, Roxbury, and Philadelphia, until his election as the first Episcopal bishop of central Pennsylvania in 1871. The robed and bearded patriarch I knew from photographs was the author of two antiquarian volumes: *Memoirs of the Life and Services of the Rt. Rev. Alonzo Potter, D.D., LL.D., Bishop of the Protestant Episcopal Church in The Diocese of*

19

Pennsylvania, and *The Life and Labors of Bishop Hare: Apostle to the Sioux*. In mid-life he altered d'Wolf by capitalizing the D, dropping the apostrophe, and adding two e's. "For tone" he is said to have said. In family memoirs and genealogies "for tone" is invariably set off by quotation marks. Marks are signals. Soldiers at a distance send watchwords across intervals. The curtain has risen another war is beginning. When Theodora Goujaud d'Wolf Colt a family poet (poetess) hired experts to trace the origin of her family name, the experts came up with a coat of arms and motto: Vincit Qui Patitur—He Conquers Who Endures.

What made the Bishop positively primitive to liberal modernists was his excessive nineteenth-century predilection for getting and spending (three wives eighteen children). He and his wives had many more sons than daughters for some reason most of the daughters didn't survive anyway. Julia, Anna, Antoinette, and Helen Maria, all lived for only a year or less; Louise was ten when something took her off. There was also another Mark Antony DeWolfe Howe between Grandpa and his father. The first one came from the second marriage. Born in 1848 buried in 1850 he is interred under a miscarved gravestone as "Marcuo." My grandfather was the fourth of five children born to the third wife, Eliza Whitney, daughter of an inventor and manufacturer of railway-car wheels. By then his father was fifty-six and his mother thirty-seven so to his Bostonian grandchildren the first Mark Antony was always posthumous. Eroticism inevitably strode forward into any conversation if his name came up as it often did behind Grandpa's back. Biblical fecundity rendered the Bishop foreign; more than foreign, wolfishly funny. To prime things to the brim they knew that when his first wife (eight years of marriage five children) died in 1841 on the Island of Santa Cruz (now St. Croix), her body was preserved in a cask of spirits and shipped home for burial.

Th'expence of Spirit in a waste of shame
Lustful and manifest in action, men in the early d'Wolf and Howe families were generally sea captains, privateers, slave traders; some involved in the China trade, others in whaling; most sailed out of Bristol, Rhode Island. Balthasar d'Wolf first shows up on this side of the Atlantic (no one knows where he came from) when he is hauled into court in Lyme, Connecticut, for smoking in public. Edward d'Wolf fought in King Philip's War. In 1779, Simon the son of Mark Antony d'Wolf and Abigail Potter died at sea with Mark Antony d'Wolf Jr. In 1791 the first federal grand jury in Rhode Island charged another son, James d'Wolf, with throwing a female African slave overboard during the Middle Passage because she was

sick with smallpox. George Howe traced the court documents when he was writing *Mount Hope: A New England Chronicle* (1959). ". . . James d'Wolf, not having the fear of God before his eyes, but being moved and seduced by the instigation of the Devil. . .did feloniously, willfully and of his malice aforethought, with his hands clinch and seize in and upon the body of said Negro woman . . . and did push, cast and throw her out of said vessel into the Sea and waters of the Ocean, whereby and whereupon she then and there instantly sank, drowned and died." "Captain Jim" already had a reputation for having slaves thrown over the side. He enjoyed cutting their hands off at the wrist personally, if they clung to the taffrails. So he lay low until 1795, when a more lenient district attorney nol-prossed the case. When this murderous ancestor could finally afford to buy his own slave ship he christened her *Sukey.* Sukey is my nickname. No one in the family, except my father, ever called me Susan, and he only did after he came home from the war and only if he was angry. To Grandpa I was always Sukey. Two people are speaking a language unknown to each other, I hear only a confused noise. Can you understand the nonsense they are talking? Captain Jim's sister, my great great great grandmother Abigail, married Perly Howe. Three of their sons were lost together at sea along with her sister Lydia's two boys in 1801 when the ship *Lavinia,* almost home, after circling the globe trading Yankee goods for furs of the North Pacific and then exchanging fur for china in China, broke up in a snowstorm off Cape Cod. Abigail's brother Simon's son, committed suicide somewhere on the Slave Coast. His brother, John d'Wolf, "Norwest John," another early venture capitalist, sailed to Russia by way of Alaska. He spent time in New Archangel, Kamchatka, before crossing Siberia on a sled in winter. Even if Captain John d'Wolf isn't the fictional Captain Robert Walton in Mary Shelley's *Frankenstein,* he married Mary Melvill [sic], Herman Melville's aunt, and so made his way into the "The Affidavit" chapter of *Moby-Dick.* His first cousin John "Squire" Howe was the "Bishop's" father. Squires, bankers, commodores, architects, actors, and bishops were a later by-product generally they only spent summers in Bristol. My grandfather, often referred to as the "Dean of Boston letters" or the fictional "late George Apley," because he encompassed the essence of what it meant to be Bostonian, was not Bostonian. His immediate family constellation occupied a large decaying farmhouse by the sea in Bristol called *Weetamoe,* until he married Fanny Quincy and escaped into genteel American idealism.

Several years ago while I was working on another essay I ran across Weetamoo, squaw-sachem of the Wampanoags, Queen of Pocasset (now Tiverton), wife of Wamsutta the son of Massasoit, and sister-in-law of the Narragansett sachem, Metacomet (King Philip to the colonial militia), in Mary Rowlandson's *The Soveraignty & Goodness of God, Together, with the*

Faithfulness of His Promises Displayed. Rowlandson was taken captive during what has come to be known as King Philip's War (1675–77). In that war, Captain Benjamin Church "Mad In pursuit, and in possession so, Had, having, and in quest to have, extreme/" with members of the colonial militia tracked Metacomet/Philip "past reason hunted, and no sooner had,/ Past reason hated as a swallowed bait," into a swamp near Mount Hope (Montaup Pappasquash Bristol) and beheaded him. Metacomet's head was exhibited on a pole in Plymouth (thirty-five miles west) for twenty-five years. His body was quartered and each separate piece hung up on four separate trees; I don't know where or for how long. Weetamoo escaped the murderous Christian soldiers again and again until on August 6, 1676, she was drowned while trying to float by raft to her kingdom of Pocasset. The tide washed her body up on land that eventually became the Howe farm.

The art of surveying has no definite historical beginning though the Chinese knew the value of the loadstone and in Egypt the tomb of Menna at Thebes has a representation of two men in chains measuring a field of corn. Narrative voices of landowners map a past which is established. The person taking possession talks of the lure and loot long after the shock of first assault. Mow(e) rhymes visually with how(e) and aurally with moo. Of course there would be mowed lawns around the house because the soul is conceived to be a facsimile of the body. Fields where cows graze are closer to primordial verbal material. During the American Revolution when the British War Office issued a guidebook for troops who were coming over to bring the disobedient colonies to heel, its author confused the Wampanoag sachem, Metacomet, with Spanish King Philip. "Bristol is remarkable for King Philip of Spain having a palace nearby and being killed in it." In the nineteenth century *Weetamoe* was a working farm owned by gentleman farmers. Just think of your ears as eyes over mirrors Weetamoo.
Cinder of the lexical drift.

"The Dean of Boston Letters" didn't write serious histories, his enthusiasms were indeterminate, he was a dabbler and a dilettante. During the 1940s, masculinity, work, and progress overwhelmingly signified to me quarreling, disconnectedness, aggression. Grandpa, nicknamed by his children "Wayne" after Mad Anthony Wayne, a dead boxing champion, was one of life's noncombatants. I remember him as tender, domestic, androgynous. I guess Wayne was a way to set him apart from my father Mark, sometimes referred to by friends as "The Last Puritan" after a character in George Santayana's novel. Mark DeWolfe Howe was born in

Boston in 1906. "Antony" was dropped as an expense of spirit in a waste of shame. To Bostonian ears the tone was wrong. In Shakespeare's *Antony and Cleopatra,* Antony exhibits both a lack of economy and positive misbehavior. If Cleopatra is the personification of lust he is under her influence. Whatever the reason proper Bostonians frowned on names with too many vowels particularly vowel endings. The Bishop might have protested but he was dead. I may have mixed up some of these sordidly spectacular relatives but this is the general genealogical picture, a postmodern version. It could be called a record of mistakes.

Irish American English

Almost every Sunday during the war years, Fanny and I traveled with our mother from Cambridge to Boston by subway. We got off at the Charles Street station. The station was above ground because it was the first stop after crossing the river. Rising across the water Boston represented the distinction between nature and corporation. A finite old world, an ordered sequence of buildings, all peculiarly blank on Sunday. Even then I knew my father escaped by marrying my mother even if he only made it across the Charles River via Buffalo to Cambridge. The façade of the Charles Street Jail reinforced the effect of enclosure. We saw the barred windows but never felons though we knew they were *behind* on secret grounds. The iron railings suggested that legal procedure is grounded in vengeance.

We walked along Charles Street to Pinckney and on up the hill to Grandpa's apartment, the ground floor and basement, at 16 Louisburg Square. After his death Aunt Helen wrote a book, more or less about him, called *The Gentle Americans 1864-1960: Biography of a Breed.* She referred to this work as a "daughter's documentary." Like her two brothers she was restless under the constraints of genteel tradition in Boston. She was trying to escape parental and cultural benevolence until, quite unexpectedly and with shocking suddenness, her mother died in April 1933. It was understood by everyone, including herself, that she see her father through the catastrophe by remaining in the neighborhood at least, her brothers had more important things to do. During the war years, though she traveled a lot, she had a small apartment just around the corner on Pinckney Street. My father and his mother were so close he confined their love to a space inside himself and almost never spoke of her to us even after he came home from Europe though I know he saw her in my sister Fanny and could take this daughter as representing his mother's quietness; a light of recognition he believed in. This first Fanny Quincy Howe wrote essays too, but anonymously. Her first published collection *The Notion Counter: Notes About Nothing by Nobody*, was followed by *Small Wares*. Though I do have several thin volumes, *Wensley: A Story Without A Moral*, *Charicles: A Dramatic Poem*, and *Lyteria: A Dramatic Poem* by Edmund and Josiah Quincy none of her essays were passed along to us; before Aunt Helen's book I had no idea she wrote anything. In 1977, The Feminist Press published *The Maimie Papers* consisting of letters from Maimie Pinzer, a reformed prostitute, to my grandmother. This book is still popular in sociology and women's studies departments of universities because it provides a sociocultural record of that historically inarticulate subculture, or so the editors say. There are no letters from Fanny Quincy Howe to Maimie Pinzer, they must have been lost or thrown out by Maimie or someone in her family. The introduction swiftly provides a standardized version of a "proper Bostonian" before hastening on to the "multi-dimensioned" persona of Maimie. Ruth Rosen, one of the editors, says "Mrs. Howe became a diary for her." What wounds Fanny had ever received, what the two women might have had in common; the courage they might have built in each other isn't the point the editors of this correspondence hope to make. "How did working-class women live during a period of history characterized by great industrial exploitation and institutionalized sexism," is what Rosen and her fellow editors are after. "The Maimie Project," as it was called at first, intended to address this question.

Maimie was my mother's nickname in Ireland, in the United States people call her Molly. She says that if our father's mother had been around in 1935 he would never have been allowed to marry her because in those days, in Boston, being Irish meant she wasn't good enough. It went without saying if the Howes were snobs Quincys were worse because it was through Quincys the Boston Howes were related to a President of the United States, a President of Harvard College, two mayors of Boston, etc., etc., but that was long ago. Now there was no money and only one male Quincy left, Cousin Edmund, who did nothing, some of the time in Italy, some of the time in an indescribably gloomy apartment near the Charles River. Mabel and Helen, my grandmother's two older sisters, were still alive, but they lost their proper names when they married, and during the 1940s both of them were rapidly losing their wits. My mother often refers to the Quincys as "innocents." Not American cultural innocents, worthless in a scheming world in the sense of being fools, but honest. No, she means nuts. "All the Quincy china is cracked" is still one of her best aphorisms.

The curious thing about my grandfather's apartment was getting into it. We climbed the front steps to the principal entrance on the first floor. Once inside you could tell a single family used to live there because of the narrow hallway with its curving staircase and gracefully carved banister; there was no elevator. This lowest hall at the base of the stairwell held the trace of another order of living forever closed to those of us coming in *now*, and that is the way we travel from periphery to center, guided by immediate experience and common sense to a new arrangement so we never merely stay in place. The door to Grandpa's apartment was in back where it was dark. Since the first floor was the second in terms of his complete living space, and living rooms in Louisburg Square had bay windows facing the street, his visitors must reach that public gathering place by walking through the bedroom, and the first thing you saw in this intimate space, normally closed to the public in genteel domestic arrangements of the 1940s, was a massive curtained double bed just like the one in the Doré illustrations for "Little Red Riding Hood." If a house is a stage for the theater of the family this was a stage within a stage because the mattress was so high off the ground it could have been a platform and the four mahogany bedposts had curtains though I don't think he ever pulled them shut. It was the bed he was born in at *Weetamoe* as long ago as the same year Abraham Lincoln was assassinated. Imagine three bourgeois women bringing eighteen children into the world on that small stage. Sometimes children take a long time arriving. Screams and pre-verbal cries vast interior dimness.

Telepsychology. We have always been in contact with one another, keeping on never letting go, no distance as to time, nothing such as liberty because we are in the field of history.

What are you crying for, Great-Grandmother?

For all the ruin so intolerably sad.

But we have plenty to eat. We are lucky to be living in the United States, so very new and very old, lucky to be in the new part. Everything is clearer now we have electric light.

You must go on as if I was an open door. Go right on through me I can't answer all your questions.

Beyond the bedroom was the living room at the front facing the Square. It was a long large room filled with all sorts of novels, histories, biographies, dictionaries, encyclopedias, portraits, third-rate nineteenth century landscapes, statues, busts, a model of the Parthenon under glass, a grand piano, stacks of musical scores, and furniture from any time frame

25

except contemporary. There my grandfather held court surrounded by all his loved antiques and objets d'art as numerous as they were various, most of them slightly battered or faded. Except the portrait of his wife, that he did get restored, so that the cerulean and Prussian blues of it sounded the note of one who died early before she or the paint could crack like her sisters. There was never any question Grandpa would marry again. Just as there was never any question he would punish Fanny and me in place of our absent father even if he was supposed to.

The thing I remember more than anything else in the apartment is an elaborately carved ivory pagoda under glass in the basement dining room. I don't know whatever happened to it. I think it was donated to a museum by Aunt Helen but I don't know which one. Uncle Quincy and my father are long since dead and no one ever consulted my mother though Grandpa came to live with us when he was very old, after his Irish housekeeper Mary Lawrence died. It was my mother who read The Lord is my Shepherd and sat beside him holding his hand when he was dying. Maybe she is right about the Howe and Quincy snobbery. Was she fatally Irish? Was "Molly" peculiarly suspect because she wasn't a *paid* housekeeper? "O Dark Rosaleen,/the trouble you're seein',/Sure they're turnin' you into a/black Magdalene," by someone anonymous is the epigraph to her first novel, *Mount Venus*.

Delay in glass

In my memory the transparent cabinet is nearly five feet tall though breakable so it's in arrest on a small table made for the purpose of holding both because the exquisite pagoda, mythic and legendary, coexists with glass. It must have been acquired in China by a predatory d'Wolf or an entrepreneurial Quincy and brought back to Bristol or Boston as loot. I don't know how or why it arrives at Louisburg Square. A pure past is it speakable? Sounds have paper-thin edges. Thus time dies and is not slain. See, deaf to us. Each fantastically carved stage or floor of the pagoda consists of a miniature room with a door but even the walls are open as a sieve is. A tiny ivory bell hangs in each entrance. If there is a sudden vibration in the dining room on our side of being, if someone speaks too suddenly, even a draft from the window is enough, all the skeletal bells shake as if the present can coexist in thin paper dress. Writing from perception to recollection I imagine a carved human figure at the door on each landing, semitransparent. Innocency. A pure past that returns to itself unattackable in the framework. Restoration. The light of twelve must be one or separate from what it merely represents stepping into the heart of metaphysics.

House in glass with steel structure

Look down a perspective of twenty centuries. Idealism a mirror where everything disappears to nothing Realism [Fragment/slash/quotation]. Etienne Jules Marey the inventor of chronophotography wanted to cut time so it could become representable. Intuition is a mirror five fathoms retrospect easel to screen. The International Peace Bridge to Fort Erie, Ontario, was opened in 1927 as a memorial to a hundred years of U.S.-Canadian peace. Some things the origin of property for instance hold on by drift or design. Poems reflect the play of light its shadows on the mirror its splinters in the *Bacchae* radical ecstatic dancers carry fire on their heads it is so it itself it doesn't burn them. The lost pardon. The good parent. Mother alone the father absent. There are so many things left out of *Hamlet*. Laertes speaks in meter everywhere. Why does Ophelia and only Ophelia speak prose in Act IV scene v? Stranger she sees more than earthly beauty. Irrationalist extant pieces before and after colonization surrounded by general rules phenomena phenomena from rules then we consider signs rather than causes Bishop Berkeley (1734) *Principles of Human Knowledge*. Nor is the ghost allowed to step forward a muffled form the only trace left in order to grip us calling collective retribution after World War I. Give him a ladder to do archival research. One day after Cold War politics of the postwar world there is a door into the recent past of Modernism. Now draw a trajectory in imagination where logic and mathematics meet the materials of art. Canvas, paper, pencil, color, frame, title—

fifteenth of October, 1764, as I sat mus
efooted friars were singing vespers in t
demon darkened intelle

e decline and fall of the city first started t
at and fall of the city

uocables

of conception are recorded:
n the close of evening, as I sat
moment of conception are recorded: f

al the place and
y
teenth of Octe
musing in the C
rs, while they we
er on the ruins of

Memoirs.

Benjamin Franklin tells us to lose no time, be always employed in something useful. He is the economic father of the United States inventive and unbridled. The essential part of any invention is distance and connectedness. We pass each other pieces of paper. A sheet of paper, a roll of film, the frame structure. Conceptual projects of the 1960s and 1970s combined windows, mirrors, garbage, photographs, video, dance, tape recordings, rope, steel, yarn, nails, cars, machines just about anything. Some minimalist sculptors started out painters or poets or vice versa. Cold War sadism was in full swing, all at large in the fiery impossibilty of Vietnam. According to Pyrrho of Elis since nothing can be known the only proper attitude is imperturbability. Pyrrho of Elis, here is infantile anxiety. While I am writing pieces of childhood come away. How do I put the pieces back?

Mirror axis

One day while riding in the forest Joseph Ellicott, "our Romulus," stops at a natural junction of east-west transportation routes from the Hudson Mohawk Valley to the Great Lakes, and pointing to the lake and river just visible through trees assures his riding companion, Mrs. James Brisbane, that a city "designed by nature for the great emporium of the Western World will arise at the mouth of Buffaloe creek and the country contiguous thereto." He renames the village New Amsterdam although members of the Seneca nation living there under British protection since 1780, along with other traders, trappers, and farmers, already refer to the settlement as Buffalo Creek, probably because herds of buffalo once inhabited salt licks in the area.

This place is called by the natives Teuh-sce-whe-aok. These lines I transmit to you from the point of impact throughout every snowing difficulty are certified by surveyors chain-bearers artists and authors walking the world keeping Field Notes. A representation of all the hills and valleys they pass, all rivers creeks and runs. This goes on forever as far as precapitalist Utopia because the Niagara River constitutes part of the boundary between the United States and Canada. Now throw the pebble farther out to the voluble level of totemism.

In 1808, realizing the importance of the location of this struggling frontier settlement at the far northwestern corner of New York State, the managing agent and surveyor for the Holland Land Company in Genesee County drafted plans for an elaborately baroque city, based on Major Pierre Charles L'Enfant's design for Washington D.C., and on the gardens at Versailles. Streets, avenues, and terraces named for Indian tribes (Mohawk, Huron, Chippewa, Seneca, Onondaga, Oneida, Delaware,

Missiaga) birds and animals (Swan, Crow, Eagle, Elk) for the most part paved, would be linked by radiating boulevards named for the directors of the Holland Land Company (Stadnitski, Vollenhoven, Casenovea [*sic*], Busti, Van Staphorst), with public squares at each intersection. Outer lot No. 104 was reserved for his personal use: "a noble manor, one hundred acres of land between Eagle and Swan streets and from Main nearly to Jefferson street, almost enough for a principality in Germany. . . ." The bachelor surveyor proposed to build his house and gardens at the semi-circular plot where Vollenhoven, Stadnitski, Van Staphorst avenues north and south converged. At night double lines of light would run out from Niagara Circle into the surrounding darkness. In his mind's eye (according to Professor Ellicott Evans, LL.D.) Joseph Ellicott saw a populous and wealthy future he was all wrapped up in it. Nervous against his coming removal he planned to bequeath this possible masterpiece of landscape architecture to the citizens of New Amsterdam/Buffalo as a place of public resort. Over his dead body.

"Adieu, adieu." Just to touch across.

In 1809 all the arrangements had been made for the building when the village commissioners put an end to the plan by running a street along the main westerly end of the lot, cutting directly through the semi-circle, and isolating the small piece of greensward that remained. "Mr. Ellicott always held that the act of the Commissioners had been illegal—they had no authority to run a street of more than four rods width. The stones were removed. I believe they were used in building the jail. . . ." Old Ellicott could even have a handkerchief in his hand, and hold it to his ear, as if he could still feel the poison there, as if it were still seeping.

Flinders

Its hard to know where to begin.

In the old days when the world was in a better frame and wishing still helped, a mother and a father had two little girls. They loved them with all the love parents feel for their children. The brute force is Buffalo because of its position as a way station whose primary function is the movement of goods from east to west and vice versa in dark reaches before soldiers come foraging. Close by lies a great forest approaching Modernism my early poems project aggression.

HINGE PICTURE

Fig. 78. VIGILANT

Perhaps make a HINGE PICTURE. (folding yardstick, book. . . .)
develop in space the PRINCIPLE OF THE HINGE in the displacements 1st in the
plane 2nd in space.

Marcel Duchamp, note for the Green Box

1.

invisible angel confined
to a point simpler than
a soul a lunar sphere a
demon darkened intelle
ct mirror clear receiv
ing the mute vocables
of God that rained
a demon daring down in h
ieroglyph and stuttering

                    lived promiscuousl
        y
                    in moveable tent
        s

She rises while it is still dark, to trace a military combination
in the sand, singing
"these little empires were settled about one hundred years
after the Flood."

                            Joseph dreamt
                            that the   Sun
                            Moon and elev
                            en Stars made
                            their   Obeisa
                            nce to   him
                                       his
                            brothers   thre
                            w him in a pit

LEAHISWEDDEDTOMEINTHENIGHT

his   blear-eyed   less
attractive   daughter)
when   sailing   sleep
westward through her
pillars   was   a   sign
of   being   born

The hounds of
the huntsman of
the emperor have
run down a curious
beast on all fours
a golden circlet
around his mouth
shines
like a star

a woman whose breasts
had not grown was cast
up on a seashore in Europe
She was fifty feet tall
and her chest was seven
feet wide   She had on a
purple cloak and her hands
were tied behind her back
Her head had been cut off

                              forbad
                              e cohabit
                              ation with
                              a menstruous
                              woman   or
                              mating with
                              a beast

365 boys
clothed in scarlet

followed the Magi
that carried the fire

that burned on the altar
that stood at the front of their army

The Gate of Reuben
The Gate of Judah
The Gate of Levi
The Gate of Joseph
The Gate of Benjamin
The Gate of Dan
The Gate of Issachar
The Gate of Zebulun
The Gate of Gad
The Gate of Asher
The Gate of Naphtali

accessible passes roman forest craggy
and the pyranees melt a moist valley
flesh and milk   euxine bulwark
the lesser and flexible strength
conducting ramparts the real their
God   and valiant magi following
white matter of the brain and spinal
cord   a long white city ALBA

silkworm peacock salamander
bee swan lion ostrich dove
fish basilisk camel eagle
taxo beaver weasel swallow
cat crow unicorn minotaur
scylla and elephant or with
herbs and trees such as
heliotrope pepper nettle
hellebore and palm or with
minerals such as salt adama
nt and magnet or with
terrestrial and celestial
phenomena such as earth
wind cloud rainbow moon

sing to Yahweh for He
is vastly elevate Horse
and its driver He hurled
into the sea Driver of
the cloud rider of Heaven's
vision dance before the
Ark awake to the silence
of stone to the feat of
the widewinged falcon my
myth my wonder tale is to
be secret to lie prone
along the skyline in re
mote fastness along the
hillside there to watch
Elijah in ecstatic frenzy
running before King Ahab's
chariot as far as the
ancient city of JEZREEL

magi   to   the   rising   sun
primitive   and   solitude
wherever   spies   condemn
I   fly   the   lonely   spot
and   journey   westward   to
Euphrates   dread   miles   to
the   sea   between   Mahomet
and   Attila   peace   most
lonely   anchorite   there   are
white   horns   in   the   heart
of   India   and   elephants
grown   subtle   to   the   ice
of   a   motionless   soul

Refuge the moment serene
repose considered perpetually
at their silent meals such expressions
as my book my cloak my shoes
Concupiscence. a handsome woman running
Were centuries peopled above even with delightful dreams
the distant hermit   the intellection of the stars

night   and   the   perpetrator
and   to   merit   disgrace
the   of   whose   indignation
walls   relief   country   of
awake   to   insult   clared
friendship   dread   rope
night   and   the   perpetrator
and   to   merit   disgrace
the   of   whose   indignation
walls   relief   country
labyrinthine   under   the
Purple   under   the   long
hair   of   the   Hun

Remembered a fragment of the king's face
remembered a lappet wig
remembered eunuchs lip to lip in silent profile kissing
remembered pygmies doing battle with the cranes
remembered bones of an enormous size as proof of the existence of giants
remembered the torso of a swimming girl
remembered the squeeze of a boundary

Antiphon
Versicle
& Prayer
foretell
the Virg
ins roll
in the s
cheme of
Things

            a
zealot nake
d in square
be running a
circle a stark
by buffeted
(sat on a
porch) numb
numb covering
qualm

five   princes
buried   their
father   divid
ed his subje
cts forgot his
advice   separ
ated from   eac
h other and w
andered in qu
est of fortun
e

a king
delight
s in War

Herod fever itchin
g skin pain inflam
mation gangrene of
the privy parts en
gendering worms cl
inging to life to
the sweetness of
the warm baths
have you cut the
golden eagle down
who ordered you to
do it the law of
our fathers sur
round them all and
massacre cut into
pieces cut apple
call for knife cut
fruit when eating
raised his hand to
strike himself the
empty palace no one
to prevent Achiab
arrested the blow
and with a shout
sent guards to
execute Antipater

clarions from the keep two ship
s against the current of the ri
ver wandered several days in th
e country to the eastward of Ba
ghdad a persian deserter led in
to a snare Julian who consumed
cities and raised a tower in
honor of the god of light step
out of the imperial tent into
the midnight air a fiery meteor
ignorant of the dark of perfidy
of torture a persecuting court
across the night encompass wi
ndows land library   Stilicho
to Belisarius   claim of the air
patience degenerates into blind
despair replied the captured Va
ndal king and before his conque
ror he burst into   laughter

a gen
tle a
nd gr
adual
desce
nt fr
om th
e pin
nacle
of gr
eatne
ss

frequently palace superstition
situate   capital   the adjacent
pasture   paradise or park   roe
buck and wild boar   a   tiger
chase thousand and guard of
some   indifferent silken vault
syrian   harbor   syrian harbor
fictive   hanging   babel   all
the tongue of Universe wild
dazzled by imperial   majesty of
God and imitating zodiac rejec
t   the joy the persian triumphs
years fleeced by Chosroes hurl
forth anathema the anchorite
column cold maintain I will be
swallowed   in   the   cost   of
putting footprints in the sand

Zingis filled
nine sacks
with the ears
of his enemies

in winter
the Tartars
passed the D
anube on ice

in com
    plete armor
oriflamme wav
ing be
fore him
    Louis leap
ed onto the b
each

emperor

s body u

nder a

heap of

slain

knew him

by the

golden e

agles e

mbroidered

on his sho

e

clinging   to   the
altar   pillars   he
was   seized   by
the feet and the
beard and the en
suing   struggle
was so desperate
that   the   altar
was pulled over
and   fell   crush
ing   the   Pope
beneath the mute
Who in monarch

Claim cloud cut in two by sharpness
of steel   praefect satraps generals
emperor   disorder in the dark confusion
of the night   pursuit no more than a
moon-cast shadow and the recent secret
departure of mankind   wander without a
guide   inhuman avarice of evening
the wood   the rock   the cave

———————————————

a darker cloud has crossed the sun
the waves are slate
he has entrenched himself
up to the whiskers) I think he has

Now frightened we are not together
that the tide has come
and covered our tracks.

2.

"Crawl in," said the witch, "and see if it's hot enough to put the bread in."

Hansel and Gretel

All roads lead to rooms.

Irish Proverb

—

a stark
  Quake

a numb
  Calm

*

clutching
my Crumbl
ejumble
  among
Tombs and
in Caves
  my
Dream
Vision

Oarsman, oarsman,
  Where have you been?
I've been to Leafy,
I've dismembered the Queen.

Oarsman, oarsman
  What did you there?
I hid in a cleft,
I braided the air.

hearing our oars where their freed goatsteps sped
and are silent
by an extinct river
O Babylon when I lay down
alert for sliding cataracts
where in corridors the print of dancing feet
beyond poise I am prey
posing in snow-light
being of human form
clothed in the scales of a fish

Count him a magician
he controls the storm
walked on the sea shouting
that he is the Logos of God
that he is the Word original and first begotten
attended by power
upheld by his mother
(a very active gesturing baby)
what if Simon Peter Jesus himself
walked among the cold stone faces
shouting NIKA
emptyeyed blanksmiling

Swiftness divination these false gods
their commerce is the cloud
so they can learn what is preparing in the sky
Artificer of the universe
Magician who controls the storm
to see you in one spot
I count the clouds others count the seasons
Dreaming of archipelagos and the desert
I have lived through weeks of years
I have raked up fallen leaves for winter
after winter across an empire of icy light

Light of our dark is the fruit of my womb
or night falling through the reign of splashes
Liquid light that bathes the landscape in my figure
Clairvoyant Ireland
eras and eras encircled by sea
the barrows of my ancestors have spilled their bones
across the singing ear in hear or shell
as wreck or wrack may be in daring
There were giants on the earth in those days
feasts then on hill and fort
All night the borders of my bed
carve paths across my face
and I always forget to leave my address
frightened by the way that midnight
grips my palm   and tells me that my lines
are slipping out of question

Divorce I manumission round

with a gentle blow the casting branch

my right hand   My covenant

was garment concealed or mask or matron

Proceed with measured step

the field and action of the law

Like day the tables twelve

whip torch and radiate halo

Sky brewing   coming storm

Faraway over the hill

when Hell was harrowed

and earth was brought to heel

how the hills spread away

how the walls crumbled

deathcolored frozen in time

Where was the senate   zone and horizon

Where are the people   mountain of light to the east

Tell them I sail for the deep sea rest

a painless extraction a joyful day

bird of passage over all I love

Goodbye to all the little fir trees

of the future

far off in the dread
blindness   I heard light
eagerly I struck my foot
against   a   stone   and
raised   a   din   at   the
sound   the blessed   Paul
shut the door which had
been open   and bolted it

CHANTING AT THE CRYSTAL SEA

for Helen Howe

1905–1975

Four Josiah Quincys (1772-1919)
Three mayors of Boston
Two Hosts of Lafayette
One Harvard President

Helen Howe, note under the daguerreotype
reproduced in *The Gentle Americans*

All male Quincys are now dead, excepting one.
John Wheelwright, "Gestures to the Dead"

1
Vast oblong space
dwindled to one solitary rock.

On
it I saw a heap of hay
impressed with the form
of a man.

Beleaguered Captain Stork
with his cane

on some quixotic skirmish.

Deserters arrived from Fort Necessity

All hope was gone.

Howe carrying a white flag of truce
went toward the water.

2

An Apostle in white
stood on a pavement of scarlet

Around him
stretched in deep sleep

lay the dark forms of warriors.

He was turned away
gazing on a wide waste.

His cry of alarm
astonished everyone.

3

A Council of War
in battle array
after some siege.

I ran to them
shouting as I ran
"Victory!"

Night closed in
weedy with flies.

The Moon slid
between moaning pines
and tangled vines.

4

Neutrals collected bones

or journeyed behind on foot

shouting at invisible doors

to open.

There were guards who approached

stealthy as linxes

Always fresh footprints in the forest

We closed a chasm

then trod the ground firm

I carried your name

like a huge shield.

5

Because dreams were oracles
agile as wild-cats
we leapt on a raft of ice.

Children began a wail of despair
we carried them on our shoulders.

A wave
thrust our raft of ice
against a northern shore.

An Indian trail
led through wood and thicket

Light broke on the forest

The hostile town
was close at hand.

We screamed our war-cry
and rushed in.

6
It was Him
Power of the Clouds
Judge of the Dead
The sheep on his right
The goats on his left
And all the angels.

But from the book
backward on their knees
crawled neolithic adventurers known only to themselves.
They blazed with artifice
no pin, or kernel, or grain too small to pick up.
A baby with a broken face lay on the leaves
Hannibal—a rough looking man
rushed by with a bundle of sticks.
"Ah, this is fortunate," cried Forebear
and helped himself to me.

7
God is an animal figure
Clearly headless.
He bewitches his quarry
with ambiguous wounds
The wolf or poor ass
had only stolen straw.

O sullen Silence
Nail two sticks together
and tell resurrection stories.

8
There on the deck, child in her arms
was the girl I had been before

She waved

then threw her child to me

and jumped

But she missed the edge and swirled away.

I left you in a group of grownup children and went in search
wandered sandhills snowy nights
calling "Mother, Father"

A Dauphin sat down to dine on dust
alone in his field of wheat

One war-whoop toppled a State.

I thought we were in the right country
but the mountains were gone.

We saw five or six people coming toward us

who were savages.

Alhough my pen was leaky as a sieve
I scribbled "Arm, Arm!"

"Ear." Barked the Moon.

We paddled with hands, planks, and a pencil

"Listen—The people surrender"
I don't remember the rest but it was beautiful.

We were led ashore by Captain Snow
"I'll meet you soon—" he said
and vanished in the fog.

9

We cooked trout and perch on forked sticks.
Fire crackled in the forest stillness
Fire forms stood out against the gloom
Ancient trunks with wens and deformities
Moss bearded ancients—and thin saplings
The strong, the weak, the old, the young—

Now and then some sleeper would get up
Warm her hands at the fire
and listen to the whisper of a leaf
or the footfall of an animal
I kept my gun-match burning when it rained—

10

Holding hands with my skin
I walked the wintry strand.
"Tickle yourself with my stroke"
ticked the wiseacre clock.

The river sang—
"Pelucid dark and deep my waters—
come and cross me alone."

The final ruins ahead
revealed two figures timidly engraved on one another.

11

I built a house
that faced the east
I never ventured west
for fear of murder.

Eternity dawned.

Solitary watcher
of what rose

and set
I saw only
a Golgotha
of corpses.

12
Experience teaches
the savage revenge
an enemy always takes
on forerunners
who follow.

You were a little army
of unarmed children—
A newborn infant
sat in the hollow
of my pillow.

13
The house was a model of harmony.

Children coiled like hedgehogs
or lay on their backs.

A doll uttered mysterious oracles
"Put on the kettle."
"Get up and go home."

The clock was alive
I asked what it ate.

"A Cross large enough to crucify us all."
and so on.

Blankets congealed
into icicles

We practiced
trips, falls, dives into snowdrifts.

With a snowshoe for a shovel
I opened the clock

and we searched for peace in its deep and private present.

Outside, the world swarmed with sorcerers.

14
On a day of rest
I went naked to my parents.

They sat on a rock
water up to their waists.

I told them to lie down and put their mouths in the dust.

I went naked to my husband
in the hug of a wave horizon rolled youngly from nothing.

I told him to lie down and put his mouth in the dust.

I stopped my children's eyes with wool
as the angel did with Jacob.

To protect them from molestation
I told them to lie down and put their mouths in the dust.

Having traps and blankets with me
I camped on the spot

Hills of potatoes and a few pea-vines grew in the trash
I nursed them tenderly.

"It is three hours by the crooked way—
or three hours by the straight."
I told the dead people who viewed us.

Then I lay down and put my mouth in the dust.

15
The audience applauded
I was welcomed as one returned from the grave.
My imposter stood up
Her speech was—forests, chasms, cataracts—
I replied—Yes, I had been there—
slept with the children every night—
wherever I went—I went when I was sleeping—
All eyes turned on me.
"Liar—Have you seen the Lake of the North?"
she said.
"Have you seen the wreck of a ship?
—and your scalp?
—How did you cross the Great Camped Present?"
My assurance failed
Welcomed to the rock of my banishment
I couldn't utter a word.
Silence resumed its wild entanglement
Thought resumed its rigid courtesy.

16
If I am Mob

and Umpire—

Who smudged

that holocaust

of negative hands?

17
I stood bolt upright
then mast through the sea
I saw my husband.

We hoisted sail together
cheering one another
Children swam in our eyes
as silent sheep.

we said. the seven stars are only small heights
        covered with dense woods.
we said. the seven orifices of the head
        are what planets are to the sky.
we said. your bones are rocks
        and your veins great rivers.
We promised them deliverance.

We sat on an island
I put on my son's coat
Above us on a rock
our daughter faced the sea.

The rock became water as we sat
fragments of a lighthouse were strewn in the sand
trees made tunnels of themselves.

There was no footing but the waters.
"We are cast away."
No footing but the waters.

18
The afternoon waned
the sun sank on.

I caught fireflies

and hung them up by threads.

My house was high and dry
in the mud.

I cut the cord
and landed on the floor

of my parents

who were raindrops

clinging to bushes.

19
In the 27th degree
of northern latitude

On a small hill

I saw a vast plain

that extended westward.

A man and a woman
so old their united ages
made twenty centuries

beckoned.

They sang a song of welcome
seasoned with touches of humor

My father stretched underneath a tree
seemed to be enjoying himself.

20
Envoys offer terms of peace
with the usual subterfuge

Lieutenants carry letters from chiefs
promising pardon

Marauders travel steadily down the dream
of civilizing a wilderness

Outcasts roam the depths of sleep
for frozen fortnights

Apostles of the Faith
shout sophistries and subtleties
in pistol-shot of ramparts

On Monday, massacre, burning, and pillage
On Tuesday, gifts, and visits among friends

Warriors wait
hidden in the fierce hearts of children.

21
I looked at our precise vanishing point on the horizon
"You can never" it said.
I drew my little children on a sled
when the sled was gone I ran after them.

The Judge's cave concealed a regicide
hairy, meager, and deformed
he exulted in the prospect of Thorough
and ate sea-mews raw

his feet were singed with lightning.

Samuel climbed out of the earth
to say "There is a gulf fixed.
You cannot come into this world again."

I squeezed my baby flat as a pancake
and turned white as chalk or lime.

Haunted by the thought, the thread we hang on will save us
I bit off and burned my fingers to keep from freezing.

I saw a woman swimming along under the ice
the language of her lips was Mute
her children learned to speak by eye.

I imagined when she lived in Eden
migrations of immense flocks of redeemers darkened the sky.

22
Anecdote of the retreat
"I will not yield my ground until annihilation"
said Governor whatever

and he shot at an abyss
with the precision of a rattlesnake.

Lies domesticate the night.

Luck in the form of a fog
might help.

Napoleon used to ask
about a general who was being highly praised

"But is he lucky?"

23

Here was the town once
but where
are its inhabitants?
Around stretch parchment plains, rawhide chasms
and cracked deserts.
That rock
resembles a man
dressed up to act in a play.
Old men stand sentinel
wrapped in thick fog.
They are watching for the approach
of an enemy.
You may search for water in this valley of dead beasts
until brack
becomes brine.
I see my father approaching
from the narrow corner of some lost empire
where the name of some great king still survives.
He has explored other lost sites of great cities
but that vital condition—
the glorious success of his grand enterprise
still eludes him.

CABBAGE GARDENS

To the memory of
Ashleaf
1955

Johnson said, that Dr. Grainger was an agreeable man; a man who would do any good that was in his power. His translation of *Tibullus*, he thought, was very well done; but "*The Sugar-Cane, a Poem,*" did not please him; for, he exclaimed, "What could he make of a sugar-cane? One might as well write the 'Parsley-bed, a Poem;' or 'The Cabbage-garden, a Poem.'" BOSWELL. "You must then *pickle* your cabbage with the *sal atticum.*" JOHNSON: "You know there is already *The Hop-garden, a Poem*: and, I think, one could say a great deal about cabbage. The poem might begin with the advantages of civilized society over a rude state, exemplified by the Scotch, who had no cabbages till Oliver Cromwell's soldiers introduced them; and one might thus shew how arts are propagated by conquest, as they were by the Roman arms." He seemed to be much diverted with the fertility of his own fancy.

The Life of Samuel Johnson, LL.D.
James Boswell, Esq.

He lost one of his shoes
among the cabbages.

Peter Rabbit
Beatrix Potter

The enemy coming on roads
and clouds
aeons.
Cashel has fallen
trees are turf
horizon thanks to myself, yes
pacing the study.
Fence Island
men galloping
whatever disaster from what
captains in their cabins
crusaders crossing their thighs in death
right one over the left
shipwreck
tumbling
down
and there is Captain Barefoot again and again
on a cliff
in a cave
burning blue lights
signals of distress.

Corner to corner
waves are at the window
light the lamp
wind a globe around the window
nobody went on talking could be talked
through lips
shredded to conjectures
of primeval man
granite boulders
a victim's blood.
A screen of history at the door
populous with riddles
sentences like flags
in some gruff argument.

Dinner somewhere
then the telephone
YOUR HOUSE IS ON FIRE
AND YOUR CHILDREN ALL GONE
One was thinking
going to bed
YOUR HOUSE IS ON FIRE
AND YOUR CHILDREN ALONE
snow covered grass
furze and broom
sullen severity fallen.
YOUR HOUSE IS ON FIRE
YOUR CHILDREN WILL BURN

The stick gone out.
Load of stone
raft of straw
a cry
pushing the dark before it.

life la

nd friend

no lighthous

marin

ere

people of the

Land

darkened

Perilous

mana

cled with ice

to a torn floor

Let my lea

ves

press ankl deep

into full fur

rows

howls a wind

ow stil

lness in rooms

sombre and slo

Blind black night
strain of a web

of spears

I plough the earth
till ruts are ramparts

havoc of every host

Comic on a tragic stage

ambiguous chants
and gestures

"Hierarchy, hierarchy!"
John-a-Dreams
counterclockwise
in a wood again
addressing a crowd
from the wrong rostrum.

Island of the Fierce Beast
Island of the Giant Horse
Island of the Stone Door
Island of the Wondrous Beast
Island of the Brazen Door
Island of the Biting Horse
Island of the Glass Bridge

A man
whose only clothing was his hair

flung a clew of twine

from a little ledge
where the waves washed.

I the Fly

come from Brighten

hook storm
seawave and salmon

Glass house
Captain Barefoot

gullet of hook

all sky

---

water captive
valley in the shadow of my hand

hook.   Oh I
body.   floss silk
hackle.   filament of a cock's neck feather

I the fly
gullet here

water captive

homeless tribe
a green-bellied sea

stones strewn
counterclockwise

to be picked up
erratic seconds ago.

"Dare I hint at that worse time when, strung together somewhere in great black space, there was a flaming necklace, or ring, or starry circle of some kind, of which I was one of the beads! And when my only prayer was to be taken off from the rest, and when it was such inexplicable agony and misery to be a part of the dreadful thing?"

each
floor
had
one
narrow
window

at
various
heights
the
windows
faced
north
south
east
or
west

these
provided   Stepping carefully and cautiously. . .
light
and   Glancing to the right. . .
served
as   Scrambling out of bed. . .
watchtowers
                                   Walking slowly away. . .
overlooking
the   Reaching the cottage. . .
surrounding
countryside   Clinging to the raft. . .
for
a   Standing on tiptoe. . .
considerable
distance   Pushing aside the branches. . .

voices of children
playing the hills are gulls
on battlements   in corbelled arches
or a thief
banished to a waste place
Strongbow in search of self and servants.

lane, bog, well, pond, orchard, tree, tithe,
vagrant.
villainy wandering around in a wrap
waiting for advantages
wizard.
wings of the palpitating wingless
through elm, moon, elf, soar
wife.

Worn out man
knocking at his father's door

am alone aloud

and my throat turns

saying

beauty of winter about Her

hair as dark
as the trees in the forest

against white snow.

The past
will overtake
alien force
our house
formed
of my mind
to enter
explorer
in a forest
of myself
for all
my learning
Solitude
quiet
and quieter
fringe
of trees
by a river
bridges black
on the deep
the heaving sea
a watcher stands
to see her ship
winging away
Thick noises
merge in moonlight
dark ripples
dissolving
and
defining
spheres
and
snares

Place of importance as in the old days
stood on the ramparts of the fort
                                    the open sea outside
alone with water-birds and cattle
                    knee-deep in a stream
grove of reeds
                herons watching from the bank
henges
        whole fields honeycombed with souterrains
human
                        bones through the gloom
        whose sudden mouth
surrounded my face
                    a thread of blue around the coast
                                        feathery moon
eternity swallows up time
                            peaceable as foam
                    O cabbage gardens
summer's elegy
                sunset survived

SECRET HISTORY
OF THE DIVIDING LINE

mark   mar   ha   forest   1   a   boundary   manic   a   land   a
tract   indicate   position   2   record   bunting   interval
free   also   event   starting   the   slightly   position   of
O   about   both   or   don't   something   INDICATION   Americ

made   or   also   symbol   sachem   maimed   as   on   her   for
ar   in   teacher   duct   excellent   figure   MARK   lead   be
knife   knows   his   hogs   dogs   a   boundary   model   nucle
hearted   land   land   land   district   boundary   times   un

THE LAST FIRST PEOPLE

We sailed north
it was March
White sands
and fragrant woods
the permanence
of endless distance.

When next I looked he was gone
   Frame of our Universe
    Our intellectual wilderness
  no longer boundless
      west
when next I looked he was gone.

   Close at hand the ocean
   until before
   hidden from our vision
   MARK
   border
   bulwark. an object set up to indicate a boundary or position
   hence a sign or token
   impression or trace

   The Horizon

I am another generation
   when next I looked he was gone.

   One may fall
   at the beginning of a charge
   or at the top of the earthworks.

   For an instant your heart stops

   and you say to yourself

   the skirmishers are at it

wearing their wounds like stars the armies of the dead sweep over.

   My map is rotten and frayed with rain

Dear Parents

I am writing by candlelight
All right so far

after a long series of collisions
had a good night's rest.

Belief in the right of our cause.
Tomorrow we move

                            from hence
                            from hence
                            from hence

salvages

              or

                      savages

at the east end of the Island a great fire.

AND THIS IS THE FRUIT OF YOUR LABOR

That the sea brake extremely at the bar
And the tide went forceably at the entrance
Saw in the sand the print of savage feet

THE FIRST ENGLISH CHILD BORN IN NEW ENGLAND WAS NAMED

PEREGRINE OR THE WANDERER

                      for Mark my father, and Mark my son

We enter the ancient town of SWORDS, consisting of a long, wide street, situated on a great northern road, at a distance of eight miles from the metropolis. It derives its name from the Celtic word, *sord* meaning pure, originally applied to St Columbkille's well, which from time immemorial has been one of the principal sources of water supply to the town.

According to ancient records, SWORDS was burnt by the Danes in 1012, 1016, 1030, 1138, 1150, and 1166 A.D.; and in 1185 it was taken and sacked by O'Melaghlin, King of Meath.

O
where   ere
he   He   A

ere I were
wher

father   father

O it is the old old
myth

march

month of victims and saviors

girl on the dirt track

yea   order of knighthood
Brim

SECRET HISTORY OF THE DIVIDING LINE

SECRET HISTORY OF THE DIVIDING LINE

In its first dumb form

language was gesture

technique of traveling over sea ice
silent

before great landscapes and glittering processions

vastness of a great white looney north

of our forebeing.

Died of what?
Probably Death.

I know all that
I was only thinking—

quintessential clarity of inarticulation

family and familiar friends of family

pacing the floes nervously

climbing little ridges

the journey first
before all change in future

westward and still westward
matches coughing like live things.

Thorn, thistle, apron leaf

throughout each scene
man covers his body

calling "I have heard"

to a cadaverous throng
of revelers

who pose and gesture
acting out roles.

It is a dream
Enchantment

the animals speak

impaled again
in a netting of fences.

Wild and tame
are born

and reach their prime

all divisible
and indivisible.

Straight or crooked
the way or path

rubbish or straw
or donkeys

Then says that
they being one

incessantly Legion
for we are many.

Sing O barren
face like flint

give hand, bow
traverse to partner.

"What's in a lake?"
"Glass and sky."

Calling the glass
partners in this marriage

glass bride
and her metal frame

inside

thread, thread
ambiguous conclusion

the king my father
divinity of draft.

It is winter
the lake is frozen over

if only this or that would happen.

Audacity of favorite children
boy and girl

who come back lost
founder forgotten, reforms forgotten

clocks dark as ever
and telephones broken down.

Crowds assemble on the plain
followers, disciples, pseudo disciples

wire fences along property lines
I know the war-whoop in each dusty narrative

the little heir of alphabet
lean as a knife

searches the housetop in tatters.

Set out to learn what fear was

little footsteps of a child
direction she had taken

under a bush crying bitterly

or nearly perishing with cold

marks and signs
I followed the track

hunted couple where they sheltered
running beside the chariots

no pocket compass or notched tree.

I knew what war was

Nelson wore a wig
and after a battle handed it to his valet
to have the bullets combed out.

Parents swept by
sheltering them I gave them my bed

watched their ardor from a hostile border
dreamed peals and clarions of stars.

Noon in my mother's garden
saw clearly on the far horizon

lurid light of conflagration

lunacy leapt to the tongue of my brain

entering the city I sang for the besieging forces
sang to the ear of remote wheels

"Oh King thou art betrayed."

I learned things
fighting off various wolves that hung around the door

gleam of a lance or helmet, heredity always smouldering.

Spheres of Popes marked ramparts
then wafted them away.

Deep river, darkness, horror
stuck in the mire

I told them worse and worse.

Splinter in my sister's eye
plank in my own

I cut out my tongue in the forest.

"Go" said Fact
wide as the world and long as time.

The City shone like stone

there were savages rough skins of beasts
sailing and saying to the people

"We have been to those white cliffs."

"Children" I cried
my words fluttered down

probably were mist now.

I searched the house
hunting out people for trial
washed the walls
and exorcised the yard.

Needles fell in strands
daggers like puppets scissored the sky.

Millions faced north
the Emperor's last Conscription
the year One.

Some craned away
some used their elbows for meat
families knocking their heads together
and thanking the Gods out loud.

Progeny envisages progeny
her cage, his high standing

"There goes your house"
"There goes yours."

Temerity to invoke vengeance
lines to an apparitional dagger.

Often I put my arms on the table
and already tired

bit into my stomach.

Flakes of thick snow
fell on the open pages

tickled the heels of even the great Achilles.

Exiles wander
and return from fiction or falsehood

thread of the story scented with flowers

boys with stones
and pride of place

in some contraction of place.

So short a time
ambassadors go and return

at Cape Difficulty
science swims in miracles

mathematical starlight, zodiacal signs
which are

and then are not

every object a window
without echo

until sleep grows to its full stature
an inward All

alone.

"We wished" blaze the old, wild, indomitable sea-kings
vikings

hearsay hardened around us

cordage.

That afternoon
went out to mark some trees

came to dinner snow hanging in her hair

stirred among the cinders
angle of a tea-cup, agitation of a spoon

age, imbecility, the walk to Rat Farm.

Elders who remembered revolution
told anecdotes of devastation

honor sat erect at the regimental dinner
escape into generalities was impossible

The house rattled with hail of rebel bullets

aerials hissed and crackled in the frosty darkness.

Twigmen through a glass
were pickets walking across.

Cold as the ninth circle of Inferno
I took a canteen for a pillow

"I can't carry the world on my shoulders."
Indifferent Justice

withdrew to a huge hump.

The national banner was capped with scalps
long etceteras of perfidious.

The Perfectibilitarians were wrong

not a single chamber in the old fabric
that was not crumbling and tottering

dragooned

I dined with the destroyers.

We talked of kings and happy revolutions

the horrible idea of immense height

that crows impede your fall.

From one tremendous place to another
treading on the brink was safe.

Wrapped in abstraction
I looked calmly at the people

the reins of my successor were absolutely new.

"Quick" I called
slowly we drove through everything near

my fir coat dragged behind me on the pavement.

How clearly this   and they
may be a lie

bed of leaves
mirage into deep sleep

forest command
may be a lie

stranger and sojourner

as all my fathers were

horned sages sailing in ships

icy tremors of abstraction.

During the war he fired echoes
the Senate stooped

to kiss the highest proof

Doom of ordinance
and alliance

chairs seem straw in the streets.

CLOSED FIST WITHHOLDING AN OPEN PALM

The great fleet of Unready
floats on the waves

concealed and exposed

all argonauts

soever sweeping

existing dwarf wall once a garden

belligerent

the redcoats land.

Immigrant ship
the hour is late

up from my cabin
my sea-gown scarfed around me in the dark

belly that will bear a child forward into battle

the hieratic night is violent and visible.

Who will bring some pardon?
pushed to the side of the crowd.

Trembling fathers futile in the emptiness of matter
howl "wilderness"

at the waste
a preliminary geste

leap for some spot where a foot may jump

and cease from falling.

Nothing else exists or nothing exists
coming to be

passing away

we go to sea
we build houses

sleep our last sleep in a land of strangers

troops of marble messengers move before our eyes

predecessors

at the vague dawn
where fusion was born

no time, no space, no motion

arrow itself an illusion

fuel to keep from freezing

a sunbeam touches
the austere hymn

of jeopardy

blown through gaps in our community
our lives were wind

the rigor of it
fleece of the lamb of God

torn off

Numerous singularities

slight stutter
a short letter

embrace at departure

body backward
in a tremendous forward direction

house and host

vanished.

MORNING
SHEET OF WATER AT THE EDGE OF WOODS

Thisbe: I kiss the wall's hole
          not your lips at all.

A Midsummer Night's Dream

Who

whitewashed epoch

her hand

knocking   her O
hero

close to that nothing outside the circle
peculiar animals

fools in twilight

for though this Somnur wood
were as an hare

her hand

knocking   her O
hero

in the castle, doors open like beggars.

green   chaste   gaiety   purity   sh   inca
deity   snare   swift   leaf   defile   dispel
poppy   sh   snow   flee   falcon   fathom   sh
flame   orison   sh   children   lost   fleece
sh   jagged   woof   subdued   foliage   sh
spinet   stain   clair   sh   chara   sh   mirac

Flank parties advanced.
A large space was cleared
and a fire made in the center
around which the warriors
took their seats.
A series of movements
half grotesque, half magical
whoops, yells, uncouth forms
RAIN FELL INCESSANTLY
IT BECAME QUITE DARK

At night we moved
        close together on horseback
                                children clutching and crying
name of a husband on each baby's cheek
                                stragglers raiding
and getting lost
        wounded trees in slivers from peppering of bullets

        I put on a flaming suit of lace regimentals
            The Great Crossing
        we marched with drums beating and colors flying.

                    Our law
                                        vocables
of shape or sound
                    What *can* we do
harmony of blunt force

                                        in so far
                    sense hidden
                                        an outcome
                                        a perfection
the world is good and distances are beautiful

                    Our law
          ceremonial evolutions in the dark

Prayers

run through our laws

"So help me God"

reflection

or refraction

of light

becoming

and perishing

trackless

timeless

in time

MARK

border

bulwark

detail

from vague

infinity of

background

that haunts

or hunts

an object

sign

or token

impression

or trace

THE HORIZON

In sight of where we are is the unfinished Capitol
& from the neighboring camp we can hear the bugle calls going all day

Dear Parents

A thousand lovely thoughts this sunny morning.
At all events I have tried and have decided

nothing especial

except a new line of earthworks
in the rear of the old ones.

Exposed positions suffer
their fate is hard but unavoidable.

A masterly but defeated strategy

to occupy a cold, bleak hill
and sleep under frost and stars.

Ancient of Days
shadow of your wing
hint of what light
the open sky
my refuge

Came there all naked
thorns were there
many fair shields
and Beauty lost
was the Beast found
descended from harmony
enduring in unity
far back in some story
heard long ago

sh   dispel   iris   sh   snow   sward   wide   ha

forest   1   a   boundary   manic   a   land   sh

whit   thing   :   target   cadence   marked   on

O   about   both   or   don't   INDICATION   Americ

sh   woof   subdued   toward   foliage   free   sh